INFJ Person Guide

Highly Sensitive Person Understand Yourself As The Rarest Myers-Briggs Personality Type

Antony Felix

Introduction

Are you an "intuitive feeling" and "judging" type of person? They tend to be highly sensitive, very intuitive, and yes, they feel their way into almost everything. What's more, they are very creative, and these kinds of people prefer to write more than they talk. Could you be an INFJ?

Read this book, and maybe, you can identify some familiar traits.

The Myers Briggs Type Indicator has identified 16 personalities that people fall into. Intuitive, Feeling, Judging (INFJ) personality is the rarest of them all. It is reported that only one to two percent of the world's population is INFJ. These folks are special, and there being so few of them, the world does not understand them. Besides, they can barely understand themselves either.

This book is dedicated to unraveling the INFJ personality. If you happen to be one of them, then this book will help you understand this rare and special type of person you are and explain how you can thrive and what you need to bring out the best in you and have the best life experience.

INFJ Personality Guide

They are tender and very good, but they can be as complicated as they come. The INFJ profile will blow your mind!

Read on.

Table of Contents

Introduction 2

Understanding The INFJ Personality Type .. 6

What Defines An INFJ? 8

What Maketh An INFJ Are The Following Cognitive Functions: 9

Characteristics Of People With INJF Personality 13

The Good: Positive Characteristics Of The INJF Personality 13

The Bad: Negative Characteristics 18

The Ugly: Harmful Traits Of An INFJ 23

The INFJ Social Life 27

INFJ Survival Tactics For Toxic People 31

One-Sided Relationships 37

Signs Of A Healthy And Mutual Relationship....39

A One Sided Relationship Looks Like This 40

How To Avoid One-Sided Relationships And The Frustrations They Come With 42

The INFJ In Love 46

Common INFJ Relationship Challenges And How To Overcome 47

Personal Growth Tips For The INFJ 63

How To Master Personal Growth As An INFJ...64

INFJ Requirements To Living A Happy Life In Our World 68

Conclusion 73

Understanding The INFJ Personality Type

Sometimes referred to as the 'advocate' or 'idealist', the INFJ personality type is one of the 16 personality types identified by Myers-Briggs Type Indicator (MBTI).

The initials, INFJ, stand for; **Introverted, Intuitive, Feeling, and Judging**.

Literally, this describes an individual as an introvert who relies more on the intuition for direction and feels the world more than they see it.

This personality type is special and extremely rare to find. It has been estimated that only one percent of the world population are INFJs. However, do not let the few numbers lead you to believe that this is a completely irrelevant group in the world. They may be few. However, wherever a person with the advocate personality goes, they leave a lasting impact.

Looking at some popular people with this personality, you realize the truth in this and the fact that they are special people.

INFJ Personality Guide

It's no wonder they are few because nothing good or special comes in surplus.

They include:

- Oprah Winfrey: She went ahead to create the best and most popular show of our time on television. Her show is the mother of most talk shows we see today, such as The Daily Show, The Ellen show, just to mention but a few.

- Taylor Swift: One of the most successful and inspirational pop singers who made remarkable strides in her career and became famous from quite a young age.

- Mother Teresa: She is an empathetic soul who changed the world with her warmth and kindness.

- Nelson Mandela: The legendary savior of one of the most beautiful countries in the world, South Africa. This man empathized with the suffering of the people and gave his life to save his country people.

- Martin Luther King Jr: He inspired change in a country, then ridden by racism and foresaw the coming of a black president for America. His 'unlikely' dream was cut short, but it came true in 2008.

The impact these people have made in the world will never fade. If you evaluate what they have done, you will find that the world perceives them as incredible because of their gifts as INFJ personality types.

For instance, their ability to feel the world and offer empathetic help; they connected with their world and felt what people needed and did something to help them. For instance, Oprah gave people a platform to share their stories to inspire and encourage others, Nelson Mandela empathized with how his community was suffering, and he fought relentlessly to free them.

Clearly, people with this advocate personality are extremely special to the world. They are the healers and a positive light in a world that is slowly being engulfed by darkness.

What Defines An INFJ?

It has to be their **cognitive function**. MBTI advocates have a functional stack that they use to determine a personality type. A very significant factor in this stack is cognitive functions. They are one of the basic ingredients that go into making up a personality type.

It is not just the cognitive function that makes a personality. The MBTI considers the functions themselves and also, the hierarchical order in which they occur; there is that function which comes first, referred to as the dominant and others following in that order.

The dominant is the core characteristic, which is then supported by an auxiliary function, which is also a well-developed aspect of the personality. After this comes **tertiary and inferior functions,** which are not as significant as the first two – they are less developed but still in use.

What Maketh An INFJ Are The Following Cognitive Functions:

Introverted Intuition

It is the **dominant function** of the INFJ which means, they are more and highly focused on their internal insights. In other words, they are highly tuned to their intuition.

They are directed by what they feel, what is commonly known as a gut feeling. When they form an intuition about something or rather, when their internal system tells them something, it is not easy to be convinced otherwise, even with facts. They stick to their 'intuitive view' almost to the point of being single-minded.

Extraverted Feeling

This is the **auxiliary cognitive function**. It means that they are tuned in to other people's feelings. Because of this, INFJs are able to connect with other people at a high level. They are highly aware of what other people are feeling, which makes them be less aware of their own emotions at times. This is what makes them to possess traits of an empath and advocate because they not only sympathize with people but they empathize. This means they can experience other people's emotions as their own – they will move in to help where needed.

Introverted Thinking

This is the **tertiary function**. It enables them to categorize and analyze the information that they receive. The information is processed in finer details, and inconsistencies can be identified.

INFJs use this function to solve problems in their head to get a clear picture of anything that may seem as complex or confusing. Because of this function, INFJs make decisions based on ideas and theories formed using their insights.

This function is used mostly when the INFJ is alone. You see, when they are around people, they use their introverted intuition and extraverted feeling, feeling their vibes and connecting with their emotions, to make decisions.

However, when they are alone, after a long, eventful day, the INFJ is likely to switch to introverted thinking to process their day. In other words, they call it 'getting inside their heads', which is hard to do in public.

Extraverted Sensing

This is the **inferior cognitive function** which means, it is less developed and largely unconscious; it barely has any impact on personality. Through their 'sensing' function, they are able to process data using their five senses, calling them to an awareness of what they see, smell, touch, hear, or taste.

It helps the INFJ to stay conscious of the world. It also helps them live in the present moment, and to be aware of their surroundings. Also, this is the function that makes them appreciate engaging physical activities such as hiking and sensational ones such as music.

These cognitive functions are what will make an INFJ be the way they are. They are the basis of their character.

Is this your type of personality? Consider the INFJ characteristics below. If most of them define who you are, then maybe you are an INFJ personality type.

Characteristics Of People With INJF Personality

We mentioned that they are special people. You are about to find out exactly what makes them be referred to as such. It's not that they are perfectly perfect; they have their good, bad and the totally weird characteristics and they are what makes them special:

The Good: Positive Characteristics Of The INJF Personality

Nurturing

Do you find yourself giving a hand to people in need, sometimes even at the cost of overlooking your own needs? The 'advocates' are warmhearted, naturally nurturing human beings. They are always glad to help anyone who is having difficulties in life. Also, they are the kind that would gladly share knowledge, information, and offer counsel if needed to help another person get ahead – they love to see others doing well.

Exceptionally Creative

They do not see things in ordinary dimensions. These people are very creative, and not only in art but also in all spheres of life. They have the capability to create more and exceptional out of ordinary situations. This way, they provide alternative and mostly unusual solutions to problems other people may struggle with.

This gift draws them towards activities that involve creativity such as art, music, writing, fashion, and so on. There will be a great touch of creativity in how they furnish their house, how they write a letter, how they dress, how they address an audience – just about everything.

Deeply Emotional

Expect an advocate personality to add not a sprinkle but a flood of emotion in just about everything. They feel into everything, including other people's emotions. For this reason, they are naturally caring about how others think and feel.

They are unlikely to be involved in any activity that would hurt others. They won't be caught up in fights or confrontations. In cases where there are problems, they will not fight or run away. Rather, they look for the most appropriate and harmless solution so that none of the parties involved is hurt.

There is a negative consequence of this; they get hurt very easily – and a lot since there are very mean people out there who do not care about people's feelings. The advocate has no safety guard for this because of their emotional nature. They almost always get hit by these callous individuals. They, however, have a natural defense for this, which brings us to the next characteristic.

They Are A Special Type Of Introverts

They love to spend time alone and prefer to stay in quiet places. However, they cannot be alone for too long. Eventually, they need to unite with 'their people'. They love spending time with 'their people' preferring a small circle of people they connect with and feel close to, usually friends or family. From this circle, they draw energy, zeal, and fulfillment of the social contact they desire.

Exceptional Way Of Handling Problems

They are not the kind of people to ignore you when you come to them with a problem. They will not solve it for you or bombard you with advice you haven't even asked for, which most of the time you do not need.

Here is how an INJF will handle a problem you bring to them.

They will not give you an opinion or advice unless you ask for it. Mostly, the first thing they will do is ask you questions about the situation, not for them, but for you to gain an understanding of what you are dealing with and discover your feelings about it. They may also throw in a personal story of when something similar happened to them and how they dealt with it in the hope that you will get some lessons from the experience.

An advocate can identify with your issue. Mostly, they can feel the path that you should take, but they will not push you into it or do it because they told you to. They will give you their counsel and hope that you make the decision by yourself. They are considered natural counselors, a trait that draws people to bring their problems to them.

Empathic

They relate to what other people are feeling and connect deeply with their emotions such that they can foretell what a person needs – or what they are holding deep inside. They may not always be right about everything, but they are more perceptive than others.

They Sense Things

When they walk into a room, they immediately sense the mood or 'vibe' in there. Also, they are highly sensitive and tend to absorb the feelings of the people around them. If they are anxious, the INFJ gets anxious. If they are happy, they are happy.

Because of this, people with this personality avoid people and situations with negative energy at all costs. They tend to gravitate more towards calm and centered people and peaceful surroundings so that they do not have to absorb negative energy and be left dealing with emotional baggage that's not even theirs.

They Care – A Lot

INFJs care too much sometimes more than they should – and for people they should not, like people who are taking advantage of their caring character.

Nevertheless, they are naturally thoughtful, conscientious, and considerate. This trait makes them put others first, whether in a relationship or even in social interaction, in which case they may do things like letting you speak and assuming the listening role.

Focused

They like to get things done and to have something to do. To-do lists are a favorite, and they enjoy ticking things off. If they have nothing to work on, they tend to feel lost and bored.

Classy

If they do not have the best quality of something, then they would rather not have it. They tend to have sophisticated and refined tastes and have an eye for detail; they are concerned about how things look. What's more, they are not hoarders but minimalists; they would rather have the best quality of an item in few pieces rather than many pieces of the item but of poor quality – a good example is of clothing.

The Bad: Negative Characteristics

They Have Trouble Settling

INFJs seem to be on an eternal quest to find that thing that gives them satisfaction. In their endeavors, they are looking for something that gives them the feeling that they are contributing to a greater good or making a great impact in their world. They are 'burdened with glorious purpose.'

This is good, until it makes them leave things they started midway the instance they are not 'feeling it.' An INJF will not stay and pursue something just for the sake of an income or relevance or anything. If it does not stir up emotion or make them feel like they are growing or making an impact in their lives or that of others, they are gone.

This may bring them problems such as lacking an income when they flee from a job or business. Also, they can be seen as 'risky' people to work with or even be in a relationship with. However, if they are lucky to find that one thing which they really feel, the sky is not a limit.

They Suffer From The All- Or- Nothing Syndrome

An INFJ will not give or take half-assed anything. If its commitment, they either give it fully or give none at all. If its love, they either love you or they do not, and if it's something like healthy living, they will either break their backs at the gym and eat well or commit to being a couch potato and eat junk food every evening.

They cannot do middle –road, at least not an appreciable length of time. This trait relates to the inability to settle above. If it ever comes to the point that they have to give or receive some and not all, they will bolt.

They Have Very Few Friends

It's not that they do not associate well with people; they do. Actually, they have many acquaintances. It's just that many of them do not make the cut to be upgraded to the friend list.

Why Is That?

An INFJ craves deep and meaningful relationships. They like to develop intimate ties with people who they connect with – people who get them. They are not just looking for friendship. They desire to cultivate relationships that inspire, motivate, and sustain the growth of both parties.

You agree with me that this takes a lot of time and energy to develop. Sometimes, the time is not enough while other times, there are few people willing to commit to such. The INFJ realizes that they cannot give you their all; trust, love, commitment, quality time, you are dismissed. It could be that their standards of relationship are quite high and many cannot rise up and live up to them.

They Paint The Big Picture - And Add The Details

They are visionaries; they not only see the picture but also they have a tendency of playing out the scenarios to their logical conclusions. This can be a good trait if balanced. An INFJ can break down the minute details of a project, which could help into its realization. However, this can become a challenge if they stay fixated on one extreme. For instance, they may get stuck on the challenging scenarios and if their emotions get affected, it may hinder progress.

Drunk With Perfection

This has something to do with the all-or-nothing syndrome. INFJ's have a tendency to be obsessed with perfection. They want everything to go exactly as planned or as expected. If it doesn't, then disappointment sets it and it won't be surprising if they ditched relationships, jobs and business because of it.

They Have A Powerful Introverted Intuition

To have introverted intuition simply means living inside your head most of the time. You have the ability to see or create many different possibilities and eventualities and even gray areas in one give situation. You are having conversations, and even arguments debating about a situation or a person in your head on the spot.

If they speak with all this internal cacophony going on in their heads, an INFL will say things that do not make sense, even to themselves – and things they may regret saying. They need time to conclude the internal conversation and process and refine ideas until they become sensible and then they can present them. There is one way that helps bring this kind of order to the chaos in the INFJ's mind; writing. This takes us to the next point;

They Are Writer's Not Talkers

They have difficulty making conversations on the spot either in person or on phone. However, when it comes to writing, an INFJ can make a masterpiece. They may prefer texting to phone calls. This is because they express themselves better in writing than in a live conversation; ideas flow effortlessly and are more sensible when they write. They may say a lot of things on text or on a script and seem to have nothing to say when you meet. It's no wonder there is a disproportionate number of INFJ writers.

They Tend To Be Very Contradictory

It can be frustrating to figure them out – sometimes even they cannot figure themselves out. An INFJ can change instantly guided by a gut feeling using their introverted intuition. If that conversation in their head votes against something and they stop feeling it, they go against it, even if they have agreed or voted for it. They will not even try to pretend. To other people, they may appear as contradictory, mysterious and complicated.

The Ugly: Harmful Traits Of An INFJ

These traits mostly put them at a disadvantage and at times cause them pain. Are you experiencing these and perhaps sabotaging yourself? You may have been thinking that you have a problem but maybe it's just how you are wired; it's your personality.

Some of these traits include:

Sensitive To Conflict

They love their peace and harmony and they would do almost anything to avoid conflict. They are always seeking to build rapport with others and expect other people to do the same. Whenever conflict arises, especially within interpersonal relationships, either with family or lover, the other person may not be as much affected but the INFJ will take it the hardest. They will be extremely distressed to an extent they may get physical effects of the stress such as stomachaches, headaches and even insomnia. In an attempt to avoid conflict, the INFJ seeks to be on everybody's side, which brings us to the next harmful trait:

The People Pleaser

They can connect and relate with how other's feel, sometimes experiencing other people's feelings in their own bodies. They know how a person is feeling when they are hurt and take it upon them to make sure that they do not hurt anyone. They also want to avoid criticism. As you are well aware, in this world, it is impossible to live a life true to you and please everyone – you will hurt some and be criticized by some. If you want to avoid this, you have to become a people pleaser.

The INFJ often takes the role of a people pleaser. They will use their introverted feeling, go into their heads and organize and reorganize until they have filtered information to a point that it's impeccable and 'diplomatic'. They won't say what they should but will filter it to make everyone happy. They tend to go out of their way to meet other people's expectations so that they can appear perfect and not let anyone down.

If not checked, they will find themselves busy taking care of other's feelings and needs and neglecting their own, doing what other people expect and not what they want to do or know they should do. This creates an internal conflict, which can very quickly grow to become depression.

The Ultimate Over-Thinker

They can't just let things be. Nothing is just as it appears for INFJ personality type. They will not just let situation play out without getting inside their head and going over it a million times, envisioning the scenario from way too many different angles. They do this to feel secure but almost always, they never feel secure, even if there really is nothing to worry about.

They Can't Take Criticism

The quickest way to get on their negative side is criticizing them. This is true even for all the other personalities too – no one really likes to be criticized. However, for the INFJ, the dislike is more intense.

This is why:

- Due to their highly sensitive nature, they tend to take it personally - they perceive it as a personal attack.

- They hear more than words; their extroverted feeling enables them to be able to sense the criticizer's mood or attitude. They are also sensitive to subtle cues and they will pick up on tone, facial expressions and body language.

Using this data, their introverted intuition takes over and they can interpret what the person criticizing means usually at a deeper level. They hear the meaning behind the words.

Even if it was constructive criticism, if the delivery is poor and some negative body language or tone is used, then they cannot focus on the good intention.

The INFJ Social Life

It's a fact; being human, we are social beings. We need to interact with people and develop relationships, be it friendships or romantic relationships. This is true even for the highly sensitive introvert whose energy gets sucked by social situations and who would rather be alone and in their head.

Considering our characteristics, as INFJs, our social life and relationships are going to be a bit different, given that we are little bit more giving and we apply a lot of intensity backed by our emotions in almost everything.

As INFJs, we are blessed to have the best traits for relationships. When we get involved with people, an INFJ is likely to get in deep and love deeply whether a friend or romantic interest. We can have the best relationships and get utmost satisfaction from them.

However, for the most part, our social life, due to our special traits, can be challenging. There are two social life risks that we face as INFJs, ones that we have to be very careful with lest they damage us. They are; attracting toxic people and getting trapped in unsatisfactory one-sided relationships.

Let's discuss them in depth and also find out how to deal with them to create a healthy social life.

INFJs Are A Magnet For Toxic People

Do you seem to get into one toxic relationship/friendship after another or wonder why the office or school bully always has a peculiar interest in you? It's because of your positive light and energy as an empath; this is what is attracting toxic people, mostly of the dark triad personality types. We are like magnets to them; they cannot help but get attracted. They are collectively known as emotional vampires, the most common being the narcissist.

When we talk of a toxic person, what kind of an individual are we referring to?

We are referring to that kind of individual who does harmful and hurting things to others such as:

- They take and take more than they give whether its material things or affection
- Those who seem to enjoy vexing you and do not care how you feel
- They emotionally manipulate people to get their own way

- Those people who just bring a negative vibe complaining, criticizing and pulling your self-esteem down with words and/or actions whenever they come around.

If you are attracting toxic people, you are probably blaming yourself for it all. However, it is not about you; it's about your personality. You are not a bad person and this is not entirely because of your choices – even though is partly.

Attractive Habits Of The INFJ For Toxic People

- People pleasing; they know that this person will do anything to make them happy and receive their approval.

- Nurturing; they know that this person may overlook their ugly parts and offer them help anyway, because they are nurturers. They take advantage of their generosity and take them for all they have – just taking and taking, never giving anything in return.

- Sensitivity to conflict; since the INFJ does not want conflict, they can be bend easily by a person who threatens to create conflict. This way, they become easy to manipulate for the toxic person who is naturally manipulative.

- Deeply emotional; this trait makes them to be very sensitive. They are easy to get to for emotional blackmailers, another party of the toxic people. All they need to do is attack their emotional side and the target gets as hurt as they want them to be so that they can have their way.

You see, toxic people have negative energy; they are psychologically sick and they are seeking healing. Like a moth is attracted to light, so is a toxic person attracted to an empath. There is no better healer for them than the empath filled with light and emphatic healing tendencies. What's more, they can sense the people-pleasing syndrome within you and they know that you will do anything to make them happy- and avoid conflict as afore mentioned.

Toxic people such as the narcissist are energy vampires and they come to take and take while the empath keeps on giving and giving to make them happy – and they will want to stay so they can continue taking.

It's easy to confuse their always being 'there' despite the tornados in your relationship/friendship for love and you stay to keep on giving and suffering hoping that one day, they will stop and be the loving and caring person you hope they are – and perhaps reciprocate.

Unfortunately, this never happens. If you stay around toxic people, negative energy is all you are going to absorb. It will destroy your self esteem and make your life experience a very sad one. If you have been around toxic people, you certainly know how their negative energy can wreck your days and even nights when you cry alone.

How can you survive this?

INFJ Survival Tactics For Toxic People

Getting away from them is the best option. However, some of the toxic people are family and very close to us and it would be difficult to completely avoid them. Also, it is unlikely that an INFJ will stop attracting them; we can't control our positive light as it shines so bright for all to see.

The option here is to learn how to thrive around them without letting their negative energy and emotional blackmails get to you:

Stop Making Someone's Hurt Or Crazy To Be About You

Sensing other people's emotions is a gift you have. However, it is important to be able to distinguish between your own emotions and other people's. Also, understand that you are not responsible for their feelings. If they are hurt, it is not your duty to outdo yourself for them to be happy.

Live in your truth and do what you have to so long as you are not intentionally causing harm to anyone. If they are sad or unhappy about it, those should be their emotions to deal with. Learn to step away and let people deal with their own messed up emotions – do not make them to be about you because they have nothing to do with you.

Build A Self-Love Package

Anything that could harm an INFJ is usually connected to their attachment to other people's feelings - and putting them first. Self –love goes a long way in making a healthy INFJ; a person who can love others deeply drawing from the love they have within. This kind of a person cannot be put down.

Learn to love and appreciate yourself. You are worthy of love, respect and everything good. You are an important part of the universe and you have a purpose in this world – that is why you are still here. Therefore, because you are still here, know that you are valuable, lovable and respectable. Believe this and let no one, whoever they may be, tell you otherwise.

Love yourself first and you will be comfortable in your own skin, just as you are. This way, you are not going to be seeking approval from anyone; thus, you become hard to put down and manipulate, something toxic people love to do.

Self-Care

After self-love, the other important factor for a healthy INFJ is self-care. You are a natural nurturer and you can't help but care too much for others – it's a good thing. But what if we are caring for others while not caring for ourselves?

An old adage goes "You can't pour from an empty cup", which means, you cannot give that which you do not have. If you give love or care to others while you do not care for yourself first, you will eventually deplete yourself and start resenting the people you are giving to for taking it all – even if they are not asking for your care.

As you take care of others, it is important that you take care of yourself first. Take time to do what nourishes your body, mind and soul. After this, when your 'cup is full' then you can pour to others. This is like putting your oxygen mask on first, to avoid suffocating yourself and then helping others put on theirs.

Realize That People Pleasing Is Playing A Losing Battle – It Will Never Get You Anywhere

So you are outdoing yourself to make them happy? You may think that everyone has a good soul like you and they will love or appreciate you if you do everything to please them.

The truth is, no matter what you do, especially for toxic people, it will never be enough. There will always be something you should have done or something you are not doing. They will demand more and more – mostly indirectly by withholding the love or approval you are seeking. You will never satisfy them but I'll tell what you will do; you are going to burn out and be frustrated.

You are not a tool to be used to get people happy. Resist people pleasing; before you do something, question your intention.

Are you letting yourself down, going against your values or foregoing something that matters to you just to make another happy? Resist! Do what matters and works for you and let them find their own happiness elsewhere.

Understand And Accept The Fact That Some People Cannot Be Helped

As much as you want to save everyone, you must understand that not everyone can be saved – some folks don't even want to be saved. It's impossible to try and bring everyone under the shade where you feel is safe; some of them are actually enjoying the sun. You should think of this while trying to make people change – yes, even for the better. Some are pretty comfortable being who they are and change is not something they have even thought of. No matter how hard you try to get them 'under the shade' they will not budge.

Realize that despite your good intentions to help, it's impossible to help or save everyone out here. Offer your help but also, know when it's not needed or appreciated and walk away. Stop wasting your time and energy and reserve it for you actually need it.

Realize That You Do Not Have To Tolerate It And Free Yourself

There is nothing good you are going to get from putting up with mistreatment and toxicity. The best you can do for you, others and the world, is to step away and allow a toxic person to take responsibility for their shortcomings and heal themselves.

INFJ Personality Guide

One-Sided Relationships

You are an introvert, empathic and a highly sensitive person. These characteristics put the INJF at a very high risk of having one-sided relationships.

The following reasons point at why;

Reasons why an INFL are at high risks of one-sided relationships

- They are highly tuned to other people's feelings. This makes you a good and hardworking servant (serving the needs of the other person).

- Also, since you steer away from conflict, you don't make waves in a relationship; you never fight or disagree, saying yes to everything and never speaking up. As we all know, it takes fights and disagreements to establish and maintain boundaries in a relationship – and to claim what you deserve. An example is when you have a partner who is not there for you when you need them but they expect you to be there during their hard times. You may have to confront such a person and tell them that you do not like how they treat you. However, if you are avoiding conflicts, you will just flow with it and hurt silently, communicating to your partner that their behavior is okay. This is how INFJs wound up in unfulfilling relationships with people who do not care to give them even half of the care or attention they are giving to them.

- You are the counselor personality. This makes you quite the good listener and people find it easy to open up to you. We go to a counselor's office to have them listen to our woes and assist us. Never do we go there to listen to their problems. It works the same way. When you are the one listening and emotionally supporting the other person in a relationship, they may never offer you the same; you deal with your own issues the best way you know how, alone.

Just like everyone else, an INFJ wants to be loved, pampered and appreciated by the people we love and care for. However since we are not loud about our needs and we do not like to draw attention to ourselves, we offer ourselves to serve others and neglect our needs for the sake of the connections we desire.

Are You In A One-Sided Relationship?

Chances are, you are justifying what the other person does – or does not do. They are not there for you and you already have an excuse why; probably they are busy with work or something important. This is just what you do as an INFJ; you want to understand others and see the best them.

However, if your relationship does not look like this, it's probably one sided;

Signs Of A Healthy And Mutual Relationship

Since you are the highly intuitive type, we are going to lean more on how you feel (tap into your intuition) – not how it looks like.

- You feel there is mutual respect: you feel that the other party (s) respect and appreciate you for who you are, just as you do them. Even when there is conflict, they never make you feel less important or unworthy.

- They genuinely care for you; you can feel it in the way they handle you. They make time for you regularly, they listen to you and make you feel good about yourself, and they take time (and they are comfortable) to talk about your interests, friends and family. When someone cares, you should be able to feel it.

- They make you feel included; they do not make plans that you are not aware of because you are an important part of their lives. They let you in their life and their circle so that you can feel like a part of it.

- They keep their promises and agreements; No empty promises; they consider promises you make to each other as important and they make sure to live up to them. For instance, they call when they said they would or take you out when they promised to – and offer valid explanations and make it up to you if they fail to.

- You feel comfortable with each other; neither of you has to pretend to be someone else or walk on eggshells. You feel safe to be yourself and express your thoughts and feelings without the fear of reproach or rejection.

- Communication channels are open; you can both have a healthy two way conversation about various topics and each person is given a chance to speak and to be heard.

A One Sided Relationship Looks Like This

How can you tell that your relationship is one sided? If it looks the opposite of what we have discussed above and the following;

✓ The only time you talk is when they are having problems or when it's about their issues: You rarely have any meaningful conversations and they never make time for you. However, whenever they have an issue, they suddenly have time and become great conversationalist.

- ✓ They take but they never offer emotional support; whenever they are having meltdowns, they need you to support and comfort them. However, when it's your turn, they are either busy with something or they "ghost" you. They may be sharing about their problems but when you happen to mention yours, they go silent and distract themselves, change the topic or turn it around to be about them.

- ✓ They are not interest in you as a person. They will probably never care to know about your interests, your successes, failures or even your pains – they haven't invested time to know you at all.

- ✓ They do not celebrate your successes. They will ignore them or down play them to make them look small or irrelevant. They may even change the subject to other 'exciting and meaningful' things when you bring them up. If someone you consider a friend or partner cannot celebrate your wins, they you are in that relationship alone – its one sided.

✓ They make you feel like your feelings are irrelevant – as if you are not supposed to feel anything. For instance, if you are sad, maybe because of something they did, they say that you are overreacting. They simply don't care how you feel.

How To Avoid One-Sided Relationships And The Frustrations They Come With

When a relationship is not working out or you sense a person is not interested in being friends or partners with you, the only natural response it to let them go or remove your interest and let whatever it was fade out.

Unfortunately, this is not an easy thing for an INFJ to do. Naturally, they tend to have an issue letting people be who they are or accepting them just the way they are – especially when they have negative aspects.

We want to see the good and we believe that we can bring out the best in them. Also, we care too deeply and we cannot understand why the other person is not reciprocating. Often, an INFJ will stay and insist on making it work, even if it's clear they are running the relationship show alone. This is what puts them in a position to get used by people who only want them around when it suits their needs.

You do not have to get used or get disappointed by people who do not care about you. Actually, you can separate yourself from them and move on without getting hurt or exploited, using the following 3 steps;

People Will Tell You Who They Are; Listen

Maya Angelou said, *"If a person shows you who they are, believe them the first time."*

You see, the first few days when you interact with someone at a personal level, they will tell you who they are by their actions and behavior. If you watch and listen carefully, you are going to see who they really are.

The worst thing you can do is start to excuse their behavior. The best thing to do, and which will save you a lot of time, energy and heartache is to believe what their behavior is telling you; that's who they are. For instance, if you make plans and they do not follow through, they are telling you "I cannot be trusted to do the things I say I will do. I don't care to keep my promises."

Note And Be Grateful That You Know Exactly Who They Are

It is hard not to be resentful when a person turns out not to who they played you to believe they were or who you expected them to be. However, you should appreciate that you now have the right information. Note and accept it.

Adjust Your Expectations And Act Accordingly

WE get disappointed because people fail to meet our high expectations. Now that you know who you are dealing with, adjust your expectations to fit the bill, which in turn directs your actions. For instance, if they have shown you that they cannot be trusted, you cannot make plans with them. If they are emotionally absent, you do not attach your emotions or expect them to care. Basically, you keep an empty book with them; expect anything and nothing from them. This way no one gets disappointed.

Trust me, if you do it this way, you will not find yourself stuck in a one-sided relationship, getting your energy sucked. This is because you will be able to identify any situation or person that is not healthy for you, see them and accept them for what they are and if you do not like it, keep from getting attached to it.

When you are not attached, you won't invest your time and attention. Yes, you can see them every now and then, if they are family or if you cannot avoid them, but you will not be involved emotionally. They say, *"if you do not like something, take away its only power; your attention"*. This is how you stay safe from these unhealthy relationships with energy sucking vampires hanging around you.

The INFJ In Love

Oh! Aren't we the best lovers huh! An INFJ is the best partner anyone can get, either as a friend or lover. I'll tell you why:

INFJs

- Are interested in human development: They are encouraging of their partner's dreams and aspirations.

- Are peaceful; they have an aversion for conflict and if it happens, they are highly motivated to resolve it to maintain harmony.

- Are trustworthy, as they live guided by a senses of integrity. They will not compromise on their core values and beliefs.

- Can be very caring people due their nurturing nature.

- Will always seek to develop a deep connection with their partners to create meaningful relationships.

- Tend to take their commitments quite seriously

- Are dedicated to achieving the ultimate relationship, to mention just but a few.

We are great souls and we are very good at loving deeply. However, we are not without flaws. Because of some of these traits, we tend to face very serious challenges when it comes to finding or maintain great relationships. We have weaknesses, which have made some of us remain to be great relationship candidates but without the actual relationships – we either can't settle in one or sustain the ones we already have.

Common INFJ Relationship Challenges And How To Overcome

Why do we find ourselves unable to forge the great relationships that we know we can and that we desire so much? Discussed below are weakness that can cost us great relationships and ways to overcome them so that we can build the great relationships that we are so capable of having:

Idealizing Of Our Partners And The Relationship

Often, INFJs are idealists, especially when it comes to our romantic relationships. We have the tendency to visit the fantasy world quite often. We get into our minds and create ideas on how the ideal relationship should be. We envision our mates to be these perfect beings who do not have flaws, something, which cannot be in the real world.

This causes us to have very unrealistic expectations and end up getting disappointed when real world issues arise. The ideal partner we make in our heads is quite different from a real human being. We end up asking of our partners for something they do not understand, they do not have and cannot be. By approaching relationships with this mindset, we are setting ourselves up for failure from the onset.

Risks

The idealist mentality will land an INFJ into problems such as this:

Become easy prey for the narcissist

The narcissist knows all too well how to role play and take the form of that idealized partner in your head. They can pretend to be this, and then you will think that you have found the 'one'. They know how to make themselves look perfect, as perfect as you want them to be. They will build your hopes and your world and then pull it from under your feet. Blinded by their fake perfection, you will never open your eyes to their dark traits and even if you do, a narcissist is always going to turn it around and make you look like the imperfect one. You will be abused and trapped in it.

Never finding a good enough person for a relationship

That 'ideal' person in our heads is a fantasy; they actually do not exist. Efforts to find that person out here or even in your current partner are futile. We may meet the person we could have a good relationship with and let them go because they are not living up to our high expectations. We move on to the next and the next, never finding a good enough person.

The Fix

- Realize that there is a difference between who a person is and who they can be. It has been said that most people marry a person for their potential (who they can be) and not who they are now. It is good to identify the potential in a love interest or even a friend. However, it is important that we are able to accept the person they are now. If you can't accept them, do not get involved.

- It's in us to see the best in people. It is good to lean on the positive side but it will not be healthy if we get deluded and dismiss their flaws – real flaws which we are afraid or can't accept or deal with. It is important to understand that, the ideal image of the person in our heads is the projection of what we think they would be. This is what we falling love with and not the real person we have before us with their flaws.

- The truth is they are not what you think they could be; they are what they are and you cannot take them in and wait for them to change – they may never change. Wake yourself up into reality and look at the real person. Try to look at the negative side; the flaws they have. Can you deal with it? If you cannot now, do not expect that you will if you get into a relationship. Let it go before you find yourself hitched and miserable.

- Collect as much information as you can about that potential mate before you can conclude that they are the one. Your extroverted sensing function together with your introverted intuition working together can make a good judgment. Using either alone can lead you astray.

Inability To Recognize A Good Relationship

Our idealism can be quickly replaced by an inability to recognize a good relationship from an unhealthy one. We are told that our expectations are too high and when we drop them, we can go lower and settle for less. You see, there is a very thin line between being too picky and having standards.

We are discouraged from being too picky, but some of us drop the desire for perfection together with our standards.

For INFJs who have been taught the value of boundaries and have models of what a good relationship looks like, they may not struggle with this. However, for those who have no idea what a good relationship looks like, they may have difficulty recognizing and getting into a healthy relationship.

Risks

Just because we are told that our expectations are not real, we become accepting of the fact that they will never find the kind of relationship we need or want. Therefore, any relationship we find ourselves in, even if it's not healthy may seem like the best we can get and we settle. This is the reason why some INFJs may find themselves trapped in unhealthy and even abusive relationships.

The Fix

Drop your quest for perfection and instead develop some realistic standards, considering your needs and values that an ideal relationship for you would look like. In her book: 'Why You Will Marry the Wrong Person', Alain De Botton states, *"All of us will not manage to find the 'right person', but we will probably all of us manage to find a 'good enough' person. And that's a success."*

Giving Too Much Too Quickly

INFJs see the potential in people and we often see the best in people. Also, we want to help people achieve their potential and become the best of themselves. We can get a little intense and too passionate helping others.

Risks

The problem with this is that we great burn out too quickly. Also, we are a greater risk of being taken advantage of not to mention investing time and energy in the wrong people. It puts us at a greater risk of getting hurt and disappointed, especially when they do not reciprocate.

The Fix

Hey, stop and breathe for a moment and really look into what you are doing. Are you sure you want to give that much to a person you don't even know well that soon? What if they turn out to be sociopaths or worse? What if the coming week you do not feel the same way about them? What a waste of time, energy and resources, huh?

Go slow, pace yourself. INFJs like to give 100%; it's a natural trait and we can't help it. However, in modern relationships in our complicated world, you do not know what to expect. There is social media where people can create a completely different person from who they really are – there is a lot of fake going around. You really don't know what to expect.

Therefore, you might want to be careful and go slow. This is not to say that you should not trust people or give your 100%. This is to tell you to pace yourself; give yourself time. Get to know people, understand them and yourself and know what they want and also what you want. Give your all in regards to this and maybe if something solid is established and you are on the same page, you can give your all. Otherwise, curb your enthusiasm and quit trying to please them; pace yourself.

The Desire To Merge With Our Partners

This is quite the INFJ killer disease. When an INFJ falls in love, we tend to lose ourselves and sort of become a part of our partner. We tune in our partner's feelings and needs and end up getting too absorbed in them such that we forget our own.

The best illustration for this is when we drop a pill in water. The INFJ is the pill and their partner the water. They give and give all their matter until we dissolve completely into the other person. We stop existing as individuals and exist only in serving the other person.

We take on their problems and make them to be our own and integrate ourselves in their lives. We serve them, making their dreams come true, attending to their needs, addressing their feelings.

Risks

We neglect our dreams, needs and numb our own feelings. Basically, we lose our sense of self. The problem is, we think or rather appear as selfless and caring. However, on the other side, we are suffocating our partner - they may feel like we are too clingy and attached to them. You seem not to have a life for yourself. This is not an endearing trait and it may scare away a potential mates.

The Fix

- We need to stop losing the 'me' in 'we'. The only way we can do this is to establish a relationship with ourselves, understand who we are, what we want and pursue it. We should do this before you find love and romance. This ensures that we have our own personal life to run so that we are not pulled into another person's.

- Stay present and conscious in love. INFJs love to love but we cannot let love sweep us off our feet such that we end up losing ourselves in the process. Understand that a relationship does not merge people; it does bring them together but each person remains to be an individual. Remind yourself every day, that there is a 'you' and then there is the other person. Strike a healthy balance.

Trust Issues

We are too trusting; sometimes we trust people who end up disappointing us. INFJs get disappointed a lot by people they choose to give their trust. You see, we are good at detecting lies, thanks to our intuitive intuition. However, we do not pay attention to that gut feeling all the times because:

- The world has labeled us paranoid, like we see fires where there aren't any, and we have believed them, thus we don't take our gut instinct seriously.

- We are clouded by our optimism, looking at the positive side, believing in the good in people. Even if our instinct warns us about an individual, we ignore it, and choose to look on the good side.

Most INFJ's have conditioned themselves to dismiss the gut instinct. As a result, they have given trust to people they shouldn't have and had it breached. An INFJ gets extremely hurt when our trust and kindness is abused. Often, we react by withdrawing our trust, not just in one person, but in all humanity.

Risks

We begin to be skeptical about people's intentions. Our introverted thinking action goes on overdrive and we silence our extroverted feeling action. This means, we no longer tune in to other people, but instead, we get inside our heads and over think their actions and assume their intentions.

It then becomes very hard to let people in. We become afraid to take risks and to give ourselves fully. We desire deep connections in our relationships, but how can we develop them if we can't give our partners 100% because we are skeptical about our relationship? It totally contradicts what we want in relationships; to be deeply connected.

The Fix

Tune in to your intuition and evaluate people before giving them your trust. It is not something to be given easily or just because someone is around or has shown interest in you. Trust has to be earned; let people show you that they can be trustworthy before you let them in. A few trustworthy individuals could convince you to believe in humanity again – and they can keep your trust safe. Find these deserving ones and save yourself from developing trust issues from a lot of breaches.

Being Too Agreeable

We say yes to everything, even for things we do not want to do in order not to hurt the other person's feelings. We stay silent even when things are out of order because we do not want to brew a conflict. This can work with casual acquaintances; an INFJ can instantly cut off people and back out from such situations if they feel like they are not working.

It is in close relationships where this agreeability and conflict avoidance becomes a problem, since they cannot just back out. The thing is; you cannot get your way every time in a relationship. However, if the need to compromise arises, it ought to come from a place of mutual understanding and willingness to work together. It should be on clear terms of; "I want this but you want this, can we create a middle ground"? It should never be from a place where an INFJ is scared of honesty, remain silent about what they want and let the other person believe that they are okay with their decisions/actions.

Risks

Agreeability may create some fake harmony on the outside but on the inside, the INFJ is at war with themselves and their partner. They feel suffocated and manipulated, even though they are allowing it themselves. It may seem that the partner is not sensitive of their needs, as if they are supposed to read their minds. Resentment may grow and start to eat away at the deep connection we have with our partners. Needless to say, that relationship will get doomed sooner rather than later.

The Fix

Being a good person, at the expense of your own self never got anyone anywhere. It is a direct path to becoming a resentful and sad person who never gets what they want or their concerns addressed. Stop avoiding conflicts are they are necessary and healthy when building strong relationships. Note that a conflict does not have to be a confrontation.

- Instead of being quiet when you disagree to maintain peace, you can practice being empathic and calm as you express your opinions. The way to do this is to listen to the other person first; hear them out first without interrupting, and then show that you get where they are coming from and then you can give your opinion.

- You can say "I understand what you mean. But I feel that..." In this sentence, you are not being defensive or imposing your opinions on others; you are only sharing your opinion – they may not follow what you are saying but at least you have made your stand known.

- Establish boundaries and never let them down for anything. Learn to say no, to people and even to yourself. Sometimes when the other person is being aggressive and sometimes abusive, it may be tempting to give in to keep peace. However, it is important to stand your ground without getting aggressive too. Do not be caught up in an exchange; in fact, don't say much. Just do not give in.

Maintaining Relationships

Our ideal partner traits can bag us a great relationship, so the problem here is not in falling in love and having a great relationship (hopefully). The problem comes in maintain those relationships.

It's not like we will go and cheat on them or fallout of love fast. However, INFJs are introverts and we like to spend time in our heads. This is okay until we check out on our partners and replace quality time with them with hanging out in our heads, plotting, planning, imagining and everything else we do in there. Distracted by this world in our heads, we may end up cancelling plans, becoming poor in communication and tuning out of our partners.

Risks

This tendency to vanish on people when they need us to be present will have a negative impact on the relationship. It leaves the other person feeling alone even when you are present – it feels like they have been edged out. Being introverts, a certain amount of this is necessary and should be understandable.

However, not many people will understand that your kind needs to get inside their head to recharge as introverts get sucked out of energy in social situations. If they do not understand and mistake your checking-out as neglect, they may not stay. This is where it gets hard to maintain even great relationships.

The Fix

As much as we like to stay in our heads, if you have someone in your life, in a thriving relationship that you want to keep healthy, you have to stay as present as you can. Refrain from spending too much time in your head and make time to be there with and for your loved ones so that they do not feel neglected.

However if you find yourself sneaking from reality into your mind/imagination a lot, you may want to reflect and assess your life and relationships to see if everything is okay. The truth is; sometimes INFJs will use their imagination where everything is wonderful, to escape from an unpleasant issue. If this is what's making you spend so much time in your head, it's time to find other productive ways to solve the issue as your imagination is an escape not never a solution. Solve it if you want to keep the relationship; checking out will only make things worse.

Now you know how to handle your social and love life. I believe from this you can learn how to create meaningful and healthy relationships and maintain them. It is important to have a healthy social life, since we are social beings.

However, an important part of our wellbeing is growth. It is important to grow as a person even as we grow our relationships. This is what makes a healthy human being, right? Let's discuss personal growth for the INFJ in the next part.

Personal Growth Tips For The INFJ

There are no limits for us in the world. Our creativity is endless and our efforts, relentless; we put our 100% in everything we do. This should guarantee that we grow and flourish in everything we do.

However, the same characteristics that can propel us to growth can turn around and become what inhibits us.

For instance:

- High expectations: sometimes our tendency to have high expectations can become a barrier for growth. The truth is that it is okay to expect so much from yourself. However, it becomes a problem when the expectations are too high to be realistic and then we beat ourselves up and drag ourselves down for not living up to them.

- Perfection: We want things to work out as they should according to our plans or expectations. If they do not, we get discouraged and most of us give up.

- Over distributing our energy to things and people, who, due to our nurturing and empathic nature, we want to help. At the end of the day, we are worn out, burnt out and overwhelmed, such that we do not have time to focus on us and to grow personally.

Because of these, we may end up being stagnant in our own personal lives, achieving nothing despite working hard and having big dreams.

How To Master Personal Growth As An INFJ

Give It Time And Be Patient With Yourself

Being perfectionists, we may want to get the results we imagined or planned for the very first time we try. If otherwise, we get discouraged. It is important to bring yourself to the understanding and acceptance that good things and personal growth takes time – and they do not happen in a straight line either. At times, I may seem like you are stuck or going round in circles, never getting anywhere.

However, this is what the path to growth and greatness looks like; crooked, roundabouts, ditches and all – ask any top achieving individual, they'll tell you. This is why you need to grow your patience and resilience muscle and learn to stay put and keep making an effort in whatever you have committed yourself to do. Talk to yourself in an encouraging way and keep you going. You may not move fast, but as long as you are moving and you feel that what you are doing is meaningful, that's good progress.

Allow Yourself To Take Care Of The Person You Neglect The Most – You

Extroverted feeling makes us to tune more into what other people are feeling and neglect ourselves sometimes. As a result, we nurture and please others, and satisfying their needs becomes our primary concern.

Even as you take care of everyone else's interests, remember that 'everyone' includes you. I know you are selfless but you need to care for yourself too. The best self-care move you can make is to give yourself permission to take care of you and your needs first. This is not selfish; it is self-love. From a point of self-love, you will talk to and treat yourself in a way that empowers you. This will be very important in facilitating your growth.

Drop The Guilt

If there is something that is going to wear you down and break your sprit is allowing guilt space in your heart. It's understandable in your nature to want to do everything for everyone and become everything you want to be. However, sometimes you just cannot be all these things; you can only stretch yourself that far.

If you fail, learn to accept and move on. Guilt ripping yourself will be a great barrier to your growth; it will tie you down in negative emotions you won't be able to move. It didn't happen as planned? You made yourself believe that bad things happened because you didn't do something? There is nothing to gain with harboring the guilt. Learn to forgive yourself and move on. This sets you free to grow wings and fly.

Embrace Who You Are

Most INFJs are afraid to show their true colors; to embrace their authenticity. They are chameleons who are trying to figure out who we should be or rather which version of ourselves is going to work out in a particular crowd; we camouflage to blend in. This is due to our extraverted feeling and the desire to please others to avoid rejection and conflict. We draw a lot of stress from suffocating our authentic selves.

It is important to understand that, regardless of how good you try to be, there will be always someone who does not like you. If you keep on camouflaging to please everyone, when will you ever let yourself live and do things that make you feel alive? It's only going to lead to dissatisfaction, unhappiness, guilt and shame.

The only way you can ever make an impact in this world, the only way you are ever going to grow is when you can be comfortable in your own skin and be not afraid to bring your authentic self to life in front of everybody. Flaws and all, if you are confident and appreciate yourself, the world will do too.

INFJ Requirements To Living A Happy Life In Our World

As afore mentioned, this personality is very rare – One percent of the world population is very small. Their rarity and uniqueness comes with the following 'perks':

- There are not many people like them, therefore most of the world is not familiar with their type and thus they are easily misunderstood.

- Since there are very few of them, finding their kind is a little hard and they often feel like perpetual outsiders.

- They see things in a very unique way that is alien to most people

- They are highly sensitive people in an insensitive world; it can be hard to cope.

As a result, INFJs can find the world and their societies a bit hostile and they often feel misunderstood, discouraged and depressed, causing them to live a very unhappy life. So, in the midst of a society that barely understands us, what do we INFJs need in order to be happy and find meaning in our lives?

A Deep Understanding Of Who They Are

Naturally, INFJs are obsessed with understanding human nature. They seek not only to connect with others and know them on a deep level. It is important for an INFJ to develop this kind of connection with themselves too. As a unique personality whom the world barely understands, you must seek to understand yourself; how you act, your perceptions and so on. This way, you get to know why you do things in a certain way or why some things happen to you. By understanding yourself, you can then find direction and purpose.

Human Contact

Most of the other personality types may not understand this, but there is a big difference between social contact and human contact, at least for the INFJ. We are introverts who love spending time with people. However, we stay true to our introverted nature and we get drained by causal socializing and meaningless small talk.

INFJs need human contact – connectedness and mutual understanding as opposed to social contact – shallow talk. Spending time with people whom they connect deeply with and whom they can let into their lives; people "who get them". These kinds of people are rare but they are necessary for the INFJs happiness and connection to the world.

Time Alone

As much as we need to be around people, INFJs need some time to be alone. They need this to recharge their energy. From time to time, an INFJ needs to get in tune with their body; they need to process feelings and the goings of their life and their world. They turn their focus inwards to get their world in order. This cannot be done when they are around people. Therefore, as an INFJ, it is okay to fall off the radar and get some time alone whenever you need it.

Independence

There is nothing more dreadful for an INFJ than being forced to depend on anyone in any capacity. We crave for independence in all areas; work, financially, emotionally and even taking care of our basic need and so on. Having to rely on other people to do this for them makes the INFJ feel powerless and smothered. Therefore, as an INFJ, if you seek to create a happy life, it is best to seek out ways to be as independent as possible.

Order

INFJs do no function well in an environment with clutter where things are out of order. We thrive in structured environments that are called to order. Therefore, if you really want to have a clear head and function at your best, create order in your routine, your environment and even in your relationships. Otherwise, there will be a lot of confusion and dissatisfaction for you.

An Outlet For Their Insights And Creativity

The INFJ mind is quite a busy place. We are insightful; there is more than meets the eye for us. We see and understand things in a very special way. We see and feel beyond in any given situation. All this information can be quite overwhelming to keep inside. Letting out these insights in sharing with the world through writing, leadership or counseling helps balance the INFJ mind and makes them happy.

Also, people with this personality type tend to be very creative. Normal conversations do not allow them to express or convey their deepest ideas and feelings. This is why they need a creative outlet such as art or music. We need to let our creative juices flow into the world in order to feel satisfied and happy.

A Best Friend

INFJs are complex with many layers to unwrap. They are not easy for other people to understand and if we are being honest, sometimes even they do not understand themselves. We need at least one person who 'gets' us – or who just tries. It helps us feel truly loved and grounded – and gives us a person to run to with our 'craziness'.

Meaning/Purpose

INFJs have to feel deeply connected with something and derive meaning from everything they engage in. We get satisfaction and thrive when we are giving our efforts to a meaningful cause. The feeling that we are contributing something that impacts the world positively is what we live for. Therefore, to be happy, an INFJ has to find things to do that give them a deep sense of purpose.

Conclusion

Indeed, you have a special personality if you are an INFJ. You are a light and a great gift to this world. Nurture your gifts to impact the world positively and take care of your energy so that energy vampires do not drain you. Recognize your weaknesses and control them so they don't take you down. Maximize on your strengths and become the best you can be, as you have the potential within you to become the greatest among the living.

Printed in Great Britain
by Amazon